ACCIDENTAL INVENTIONS

The Chance Discoveries That Changed Our Lives

BY BIRGIT KROLS

INSIGHT  EDITIONS

San Rafael, California

INSIGHT  EDITIONS

PO Box 3088
San Rafael, CA 94912
www.insighteditions.com

First published in the United States in 2012 by Insight Editions.
Copyright © 2009 by Tectum Publishers NV

Library of Congress Cataloging-in-Publication Data available.

ISBN: 978-1-60887-073-8

Originally published by Tectum Publishers NV

Photo credits: All images © Corbis, except pages 14–15, 38–39, 41, 99, 107, 118–119, which are © Getty Images; and product images are © iStockphoto, except pages 1, 3, 7, 12, 13, 16, 21, 22, 24, 29–32, 34, 36, 47, 48, 52, 54, 57, 58, 60, 62, 66, 69, 72, 74, 78, 80, 88, 92, 94, 104, 106, 111, 112, 114, 116, 124, 125, 126, 128, 130, 132, 134, 139, 141, 142, 144, 146, 154, 158, 163, 165, which are © Dreamstime.

Band-Aids® is a registered trademark of the Johnson & Johnson Corporation. Bubble Wrap® is a registered trademark of Sealed Air Corporation. Coca-Cola® is a registered trademark of Coca-Cola® Company. eBay® is a registered trademark of eBay Inc. Frisbee® is a Registered Trademark of © Wham-o Inc. Kellogg's Corn Flakes® is a registered trademark of Kellog NA Co. Kleenex® is a registered trademark Kimberly-Clark Corporation. Play-Doh® is a registered trademark of Hasbro Inc. Popsicle® is a registered trademarks of the Unilever Group of Companies. Post-it® and Scotchgard™ are registered trademarks of 3M. Silly Putty® is a registered trademark of Crayola LLC. Slinky® is a registered trademark of Poof-Slinky, Inc. Teflon® is a registered trademark of DuPont. VELCRO® is a registered trademark of Velcro Industries B. V. Viagra is a registered trademark of Pfizer Inc.

Interior design by Gunter Segers

ROOTS of PEACE   REPLANTED PAPER

Insight Editions, in association with Roots of Peace, will plant two trees for each tree used in the manufacturing of this book. Roots of Peace is an internationally renowned humanitarian organization dedicated to eradicating land mines worldwide and converting war-torn lands into productive farms and wildlife habitats. Together, we will plant two million fruit and nut trees in Afghanistan and provide farmers there with the skills and support necessary for sustainable land use.

Manufactured in China by Insight Editions

10 9 8 7 6 5 4 3 2 1

Contents

6　Intro

① ENTERTAINMENT

10　Silly Putty
12　Play-Doh
16　Fireworks
18　Roller Skates
22　Teddy Bear
24　Piggy Bank
28　Slinky
32　Frisbee
34　Hot-Air Balloon
36　Roulette

② FOOD & DRINKS

40　Popsicle
42　Artificial Sweeteners
44　Coca-Cola
46　Potato Chips
48　Ice-Cream Cone
52　Sandwich
54　Corn Flakes
56　Peanut Butter
58　Cheese
60　Chocolate Chip Cookies
62　Doughnut Hole
64　Maple Syrup
66　Tea
68　Tea Bag
70　Bread
72　Microwave Oven
74　Brandy

③ MEDICINE

78　X-Rays
80　LSD
84　Penicillin
88　Stethoscope
90　Viagra
92　Band-Aids
94　Rubber Gloves

④ EVERYDAY LIFE

98　Superglue
100　Post-its
104　Safety Glass
106　Flashlight
110　Kleenex
112　Matches
116　Rear-View Mirror
120　Guide Dog
124　Velcro
126　Blotting Paper
128　Abstract Art
130　eBay
132　World Wide Web
134　Phonograph
138　Typewriter
140　Bubble Wrap
142　Teflon
144　Cellophane
146　Stainless Steel
148　Wire Coat Hanger

⑤ SUBSTANCES

152　TNT
154　Radioactivity
158　Vulcanized Rubber
160　Scotchgard
162　Synthetic Dyes
164　Dynamite

"Accident is
the name of
the greatest
of all inventors."

–Mark Twain (1835–1910),
American author

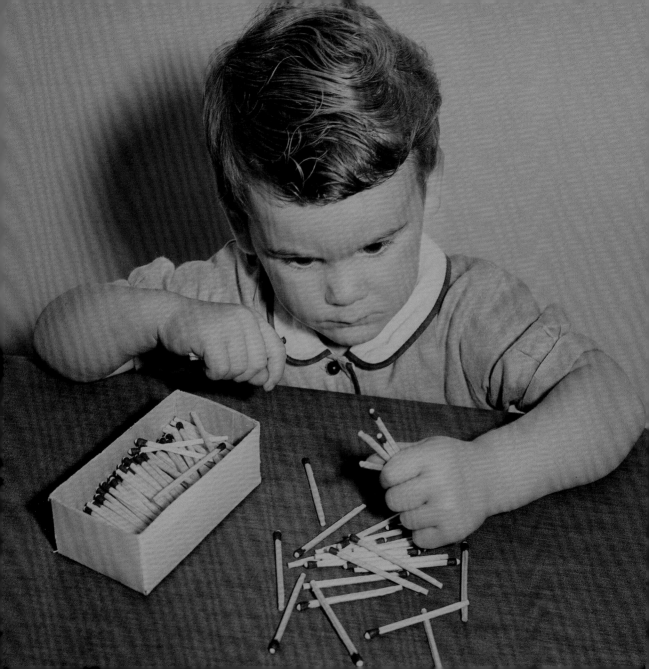

Intro

Serendipity: "Trying to find a needle in a haystack and tumbling out with a beautiful country girl."
—Dutch researcher Pek Van Andel

Some ideas come naturally, many inventions are the result of serious brainwaves, most discoveries are the result of years of dedicated research, and then there are those resulting from a mere fluke, through laziness, absent-mindedness, or carelessness. Apparently, this happens so frequently that there is a word for it: serendipity.

It was the Englishman Horace Walpole who, in 1754, invented the word based on the title of a Persian fairy tale, "The Three Princes of Serendib." The trio embarked on a perilous journey by foot through the dessert and survived only thanks to their "accidental" knowledge, gained by keeping their eyes open and ears cocked. Today, *serendipity* refers to finding something unexpected and useful when you were actually looking for something completely different. It is important that serendipity should involve not only a lucky coincidence but also cleverness and intelligence to lead to practical discoveries.

The way something was invented does not really matter in the end, and the origin of an invention does not devalue its ingenuity. But as many stories in this book will reveal, the journey there is often amazing, hilarious, fascinating, or original.

Silly Putty

1943

In the early forties, James Wright wasn't entirely sure what to think of the elastic substance he obtained after mixing boric acid and silicone oil. During his search for synthetic rubber for its use in car tires, the General Electric engineer had stumbled upon a "solid liquid" that could bounce, be torn into pieces, be stretched, could transfer newspaper images, and vaporized when exposed to air for an extended period of time. Not entirely the perfect features for a car tire. What *could* it be used for, then? In 1950, PR man Peter Hodgson found the solution when he started selling the substance wrapped in plastic eggs as children's toys; Silly Putty quickly became one of the world's first hypes. Thus far, 300 million eggs have been sold worldwide, and 20,000 are still selling like hotcakes every day.

Play-Doh

1956

"Could you pass me the plasticine, please? There's a mark on the wall." Believe it or not, Play-Doh was launched by soap factory Kutol Products, before World War II, as a cleaning product for wallpaper. In 1955, owner Joseph McVicker gave his sister-in-law, a nursery school teacher, a piece when she told him that traditional modeling clay was too messy and solid for small children's hands. The nontoxic, washable, and permanently soft clay substance was an enormous success in her classroom. A year later, the cleaning product was relaunched as a children's toy and McVicker was a millionaire. Currently, 95 million pots of Play-Doh are still sold every year.

Fireworks

According to legend, fireworks were the result of the actions of a careless Chinese army chef who lived 2,000 years ago. When he tried to spice up dinner one evening using saltpeter (then used instead of salt), he accidentally spilled some on the fire. He was surprised to see that the combination of saltpeter, charcoal, and sulfur created a blue-purple flame. Excitedly, he spooned the mixture into a bamboo pole that, once lit, exploded with a loud bang. People were initially petrified of the sound but later started using this invention to drive away evil spirits. Later on, fireworks were used in warfare, until the aesthetic aspect took precedence and it became a symbol of prosperity and luck.

Roller Skates

1760

Roller skates made their first appearance in a rather "awkward" manner at a London fancy-dress ball. When Belgian instrument maker Joseph Merlin tried to steal the show in an outfit finished with a violin and self-made shoes on metal wheels, he managed to give himself a spectacular introduction rolling in while playing. As he hadn't entirely worked out how to keep his balance or change direction, his grand entrance was soon disrupted when he ran into a wall-to-wall mirror. His example was followed only toward the end of the next century, when new techniques were being invented to make the rolling shoe maneuverable. Roller skates evolved from a pleasurable pastime in the nineteenth century to an Olympic sport in the late twentieth century.

Teddy Bear

1902

The teddy bear owes his name to a failed bear hunt. In 1902, President Theodore "Teddy" Roosevelt was invited on a hunting party that ended after three long and frustrating days, when he refused to shoot an old, wounded bear that had been tied down. When shopkeeper Morris Michtom saw a political cartoon about this incident, it occurred to him to make a stuffed bear, call him Teddy, and place him in his toy shop window to attract attention.

People immediately swarmed the shop to buy the bear, and his wife started sewing copies. When Michtom wrote to Roosevelt, asking permission to use the name Teddy, the president answered, "I don't think my name will mean much to the bear business, but you're welcome to it!" He was clearly wrong, because the teddy bear became known all over the world, assisted by the introduction of Steiff bears during the same period.

Piggy Bank

Squirrels collect nuts. Dogs bury bones. Camels store supplies of fat in their humps. Pigs don't do any of the above. They are not interested in collecting, burying, or storing. So why do we keep our money in a piggy bank? The history of this gadget dates back to the fifteenth century, when pots were made of a cheap orange clay called *pygg* in Middle English. In those days, people saved money in these pots, named after the clay. Hundreds of years later, everyone had forgotten that *pygg* had referred to the material, and when an English potter was asked to make piggy banks, he produced pots in the shape of pigs—much to the delight of children.

"It is better to be lucky than smart."

—American proverb

Slinky

1943

The first word that escaped naval engineer Richard James's mouth in 1943 when he dropped a spring that kept "stepping" away from him was probably slightly stronger than "Eureka!" Luckily, he was able to see the humor of it and was struck by the idea of making the spring into a toy. While he fine-tuned the spring, looking for the best metal and ideal measurements, his wife Betty came up with the name. Although the couple initially had doubts about the Slinky, it became an instant hit during the Christmas period of 1945. In the next 60 years, 300 million Slinkies were sold, and even today, children still don't get tired of watching the spring move effortlessly down the stairs.

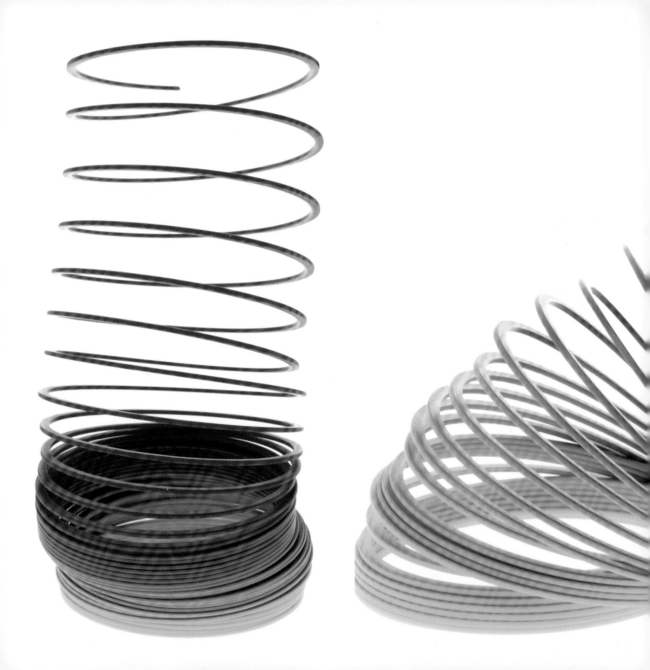

Frisbee

1871

The world-famous Frisbie Baking Company, in Connecticut, is strangely enough famous not for its quality pies but rather for its pie tins. Shortly after the company was founded in 1871, students in New England realized that the aluminum pie tins, which had the name Frisbie embossed in them, could be thrown through the air, offering hours of entertainment. In 1948, Walter Morrison launched the Flying-Saucer, the first commercial flying disk. The real success came in 1957, when Wham-O brought a later model on the market called Frisbee in honor of the original pie tin. Frisbee has since developed from a pleasant pastime to a serious sport.

Hot-Air Balloon

1783

If we are to believe the legend, it was a petticoat that provided the impetus to conquer the air. Jacques-Étienne Montgolfier allegedly became inspired when he saw how his wife's petticoat ballooned and slightly lifted up due to the warm air when it was hanging above a fire to dry. Together with his brother Joseph-Michel, he started to experiment, and in June 1783, they launched the first fabric bag using a pan of smoldering charcoal. Only five months later, on November 21, 1783, Jean-François Pilatre de Rozier and François Laurent-le Vieux d'Arlandes became the first air heroes when they took off on a 25-minute balloon ride above Paris.

Roulette

Some historians believe that roulette has its origins in Tibet; others argue that they are embedded in ancient Rome. In reality, there is no certainty about how the game came into existence. However, the person associated with this most is the French mathematician Blaise Pascal. In 1655, he apparently discovered the roulette wheel by accident in his search for a perpetual motion machine. When he didn't succeed, one of his colleagues proposed to turn his design into a game of chance. If this is true, it was a masterstroke: Roulette took over the world as the king of casino games and is still the most recognizable symbol for gambling worldwide.

②FOOD &

DRINKS

Popsicle

That forgetfulness is able to generate something after all was proven by Frank Epperson, from San Francisco. When he was 11, he mixed a drink from soda powder and water but forgot it outside on the porch, with the stirrer still in it. That night, the local temperature dropped to an all-time low, and the next morning Frank was holding the world's first ice pop. At 29, he started selling his invention as Epsicle Ice Pops. Two years and a name change to Popsicle later, he sold his company for a fortune. The Popsicle is still a favorite snack of children all over the world.

Artificial Sweeteners

1879–1965

The most popular artificial sweeteners in the world were all discovered as a result of scientists ignoring all health and safety rules. In 1879, German chemist Constantin Fahlberg discovered saccharin by licking an unknown substance that he had spilled on his hand; in 1937, American graduate student Michael Sveda came across cyclamate when he lit a cigarette that tasted sweet after conducting an experiment; and in 1965, American chemist James M. Schlatter came in contact with aspartame after licking his finger to pick up a sheet of paper.

Coca-Cola

1886

Druggist John Pemberton had already concocted several medicinal syrups and tonics when he invented Pemberton's French Wine Coca, a remedy against headaches made from red wine, coca leaves, and kola nuts. That same year, Atlanta prohibited the sale of alcohol, leaving him stuck with an illegal supply of drinks. In his search for a new miracle drink, Pemberton created a watered-down syrup in May 1886. The result was a success. However, only after he accidentally used carbonated water instead of natural mineral water to make a second glass did he start to consider selling the product as a soft drink rather than a medicine. Today, Coca-Cola is one of the most popular drinks in the world.

Potato Chips

A restaurant patron's complaint about the size of potato slices, and a chef who took great offense, resulted in the popularization of potato chips in 1853. When an unhappy customer at Moon's Lake House, in Saratoga Springs, New York, kept complaining that his potatoes were too chunky and thick, irascible George Crum cut the potatoes wafer thin, baked them until they were crunchy, and covered them in salt.

When the patron was served, he was delighted, rather than perturbed, and finished every last crumb on his plate. Crum's retaliatory concoction was the start of a resounding success: His "Saratoga Chips"—not the earliest recorded introduction of potato chips but the first well-publicized one—became a local delicacy until an enterprising businessman named Herman Lay commercialized the product during the Prohibition era. More than 150 years after its invention, the potato chip is worth a third of the global snack market.

Ice-Cream Cone

1904 It is debatable who invented the first ice-cream cone, but the nicest story is undoubtedly that describing what occured at the World's Fair in St. Louis in 1904, when fate helped ice cream and waffles team up. One excruciatingly hot day, a Persian-waffle seller and an ice-cream seller had adjoining stalls. While the first one sold next to nothing, the other was doing excellent business and soon had no dishes left. His neighbor saved the day with an invention that was both simple and ingenius: He took one of his *zalabia* waffles and shaped it into a cone in which the ice cream could be scooped. The accidental invention was such a success with exhibition visitors that other ice-cream sellers soon followed suit. The cone became the best-known product of the World's Fair and started a triumphal march around the world.

"An amazing invention – but who would ever want to use one?"

—American President Rutherford B. Hayes, after having made a call from Washington, DC, to Pennsylvania with Alexander Graham Bell's telephone in 1876.

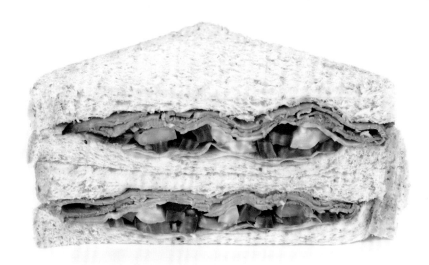

Sandwich

1762

John Montagu, the fourth earl of Sandwich, is not the inventor of the sandwich but has lent his name to it. According to the legend, Lord Sandwich was a keen card player who often became so absorbed in the game that he did not find the time to eat.

In 1762, when his servants were finally able to persuade him to dine after a 24-hour card-playing session, he ordered them to put the meat between two slices of bread so he still had one hand left to play with. Other members of the nobility soon started ordering "the same as Sandwich." The word stuck, and today, food consisting of two slices of bread with a filling is commonly known as a sandwich.

Corn Flakes

What is the best thing that vegetarianism has contributed to the world? *Corn Flakes!* Crunchy corn flakes were invented on August 8, 1894, by brothers John Harvey Kellogg and William Keith Kellogg of the radical Battle Creek Sanitarium. During their search for easily digestible meat replacements, the strict vegetarians were boiling and crushing grains of wheat when they were called away. When they returned, the dough was hard and fell apart. As they couldn't afford to throw it all away, they decided to bake the flakes and serve them to their patients as they were. They later experimented with other varieties such as corn. Pleas from ex-patients to also sell the products outside the sanitarium persuaded them four years later to start up a small business. Today, billions of people enjoy breakfast eating corn flakes or other breakfast cereals from Kellogg's or others.

Peanut Butter

1890

Opinions differ about who invented peanut butter. The Aztecs ate a paste made from crushing peanuts, and peanut paste has been prepared ever since. However, in 1890, an anonymous doctor from St. Louis who promoted it as a source of protein for people with bad teeth who could no longer chew meat persuaded food-processing businessman George A. Bayle Jr. to automate the production process.

Soon thereafter, vegetarians John Harvey Kellogg and William Keith Kellogg began to serve peanut butter to patients at their Battle Creek Sanitarium. It was surprisingly successful, and John Harvey Kellogg patented their process and, a few years later, set up the Sanitas Nut Company to sell their "nut butter" and other products to grocers. These days, peanut butter is a popular spread not only in the United States but also in Canada, the Netherlands, Turkey, and the United Kingdom.

Cheese

According to a popular theory, cheese was invented by a nomadic tribe in South Asia or the Middle East between 8000 and 3000 BC. Perhaps a Bedouin was traveling through the desert when he witnessed a small miracle: The milk he had taken with him in a bag made from a cow's stomach had changed into a solid substance. Three elements were responsible for this: the bacteria contained in the cow's stomach, the constant motion, and the heat from the sun. As cheese has a long shelf life, the invention was immediately seized as an opportunity to store milk for times of scarcity. The process of cheese making has not changed throughout all those years.

Chocolate Chip Cookies

1930

In 1930, Ruth Wakefield of the Toll House Inn, in Massachusetts, accidentally invented cookies containing chocolate chips. When baking her favorite chocolate cookie, she noticed that she had run out of baking chocolate. Therefore, she broke a Nestle milk chocolate bar into small pieces and mixed it with the dough. However, the pieces didn't melt but became slightly gooey. Luckily, the "failed" cookies were incredibly popular with her guests and even became famous on a national level. When Andrew Nestle noticed that his chocolate sales were dramatically increasing, he offered Wakefield a lifelong supply of chocolate in exchange for the privilege to print her recipe on the packaging. This only increased the popularity of America's favorite type of cookie.

Doughnut Hole

1847

A doughnut is not a doughnut without its hole. However, the hole was invented long after the doughnut was introduced by Dutch immigrants in America. According to the legend, it was Captain Hansen Gregory, from Maine, who was responsible for the typical look of this American product. A heroic story tells us how, in 1847, he speared his doughnut on one of the handles of his steering wheel to free up his hands (and keep his snack safe) during a storm. According to a slightly more modest version, he decided as a 16-year-old cabin boy to cut out the often raw and unappetizing center of the bun using the lid of a pepper box. Whatever version may be true, the doughnut with a hole was an immediate success and is known worldwide today under several names.

Maple Syrup

1620

According to an American Indian legend, maple syrup was invented by a squaw who was bone idle. One winter evening, the Iroquois warrior Woksis sank his tomahawk into the trunk of a maple tree. When he took it out in the morning to go hunting, his wife, Moqua, noticed sap running from the incision as it became warmer and sunnier. She decided to save herself a trip to the river and catch some to use for dinner. As the sap stewed, it quickly thickened into a syrup, adding such a sweet taste to the food that Woksis eventually broke the saucepan trying to lick every last drop. Maple syrup became a national product of Canada, where it is usually eaten with waffles and pancakes, as it is in the United States, where it is also harvested. Other countries mainly use the syrup as a healthy sugar replacement.

Tea

2737 BC

According to an old Chinese legend, it was Emperor Shen Nung who invented tea in 3000 BC. He was not only a charismatic leader but also a scientist who insisted on drinking water being boiled before use. One day, when he was visiting a remote part of his empire, his servants were boiling water for him. The wind blew a few leaves of a bush in, which colored the water and spread an aromatic scent. The curious emperor decided to try the brew, and the rest is history.

True or not, the first written record of tea does appear in Shen Nung's book on pharmacy and herbs, the *Pen Ts'ao*, from 2737 BC. Today, tea is, next to water, the most popular drink in the world.

Tea Bag

1904

The New York tea trader Thomas Sullivan wanted to cut costs when, in 1904, he started using hand-sewn silk bags instead of traditional tin cans to send his samples. His customers were delighted not only with his tea but also with the bags. Fully oblivious to the fact that they were meant to take the tea out, they discovered that depositing the bags in a pot was far easier than fishing tea leaves out later. Sullivan never sold loose tea leaves again. He was overwhelmed by the requests for tea bags. Currently, tea bags account for approximately 95 percent of the tea sales in the Western world.

Bread

4000
BC

Even the invention of bread, attributed by some to Hebrews, was accidental. A chef who was making a mixture of flour and water, presumably left his kitchen briefly. When he returned a few hours later, he discovered the dough had risen. As he didn't want to waste it, he decided to bake it on a hot stone. The result was a tasty light bake that took the world by storm.

Microwave Oven

1945

The invention of the microwave came as a result of a melting piece of chocolate. In 1942, when Percy Spencer, of the American company Raytheon, walked past a radar unit, the chocolate bar in his pocket suddenly transformed into a sticky mess. Spencer immediately thought of the radiation of the microwave in the installation and started to experiment with different food items. He found out that microwaves are able to actuate water molecules in food to such an extent that they create warmth. Furthermore, they have the ability to heat substances more quickly than any traditional oven. Raytheon's first commercial microwave, which was nearly 6 feet high and weighed about 750 pounds, took shape in 1947. It would take a further 20 years to develop a table-size model. These days, every new kitchen comes with a microwave as a standard appliance.

Brandy

11TH
CENTURY

Hats off to the Dutch! It is largely due to them that we are now able to enjoy brandy such as cognac and armagnac. Ever since the tenth century, French wines had been exported to northern Europe using Dutch vessels. In order to reduce export taxes during transport, safeguard the quality of the wine, and limit the volume, a Dutch pharmacist invented a process to concentrate wine by heating it up and later diluting it to re-create wine. This changed the flavor dramatically and made the watered-down wine undrinkable. On the other hand, the much stronger and more concentrated liquid that was transported in oak barrels was far better tasting than the original wine. The distillate was therefore renamed brandywine, or brandy, derived from the Dutch word *brandewijn* meaning "burnt wine."

③ MEDICIN

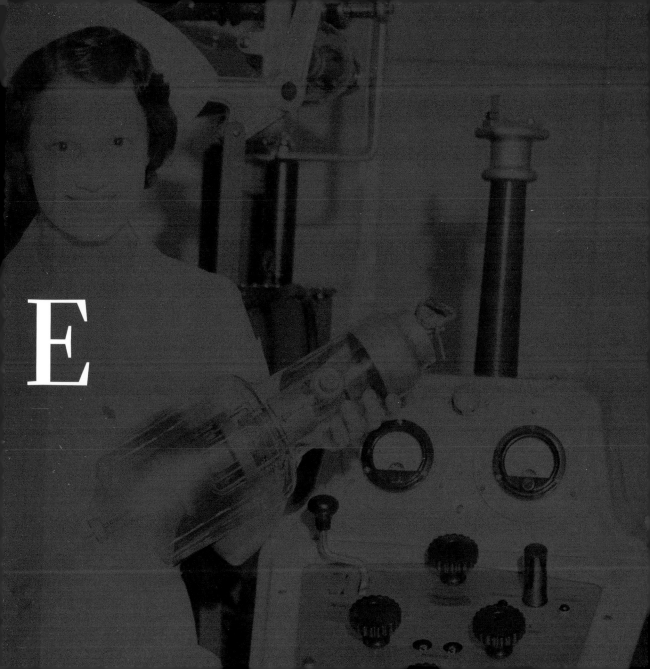

E

X-Rays

1895

The fact that doctors are able to look through our skin using X-rays is all due to the carelessness of the German physicist Wilhelm Conrad Röntgen. He discovered the strange radiation when he was experimenting in 1895, as were many of his colleagues, with an electron tube. During one of these experiments, after he had wrapped the tube in black cardboard, he noticed a curious glow coming from a fluorescent screen on the other side of his laboratory. The glow indicated a new type of invisible radiation that was able to pass through everything except the densest materials. The biggest surprise of all came when, during one of his experiments with different materials, he accidentally held his hand in front of the beam, and the bones were projected onto the wall behind him. Röntgen called his discovery X-rays, after the mathematical symbol for the great unknown. X-rays are still used as a medical tool.

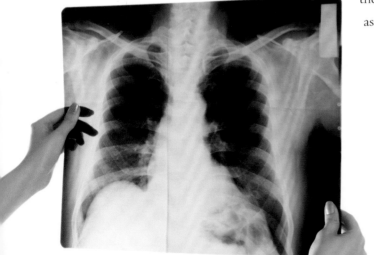

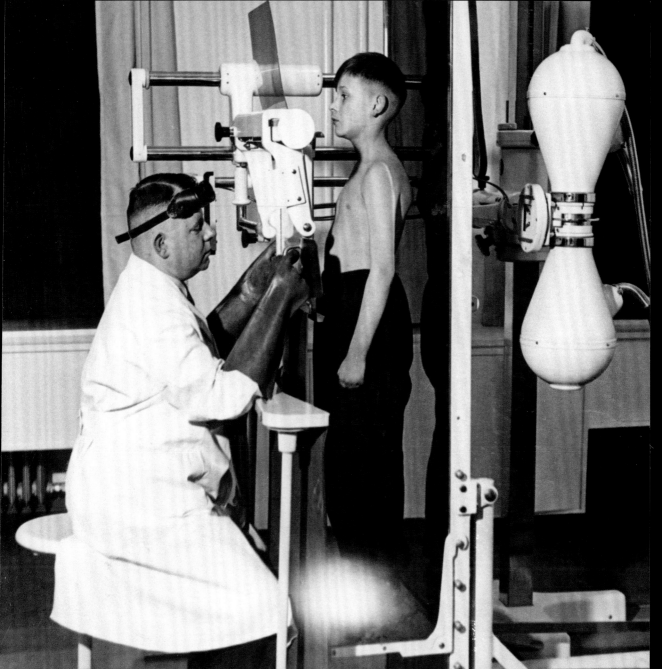

LSD

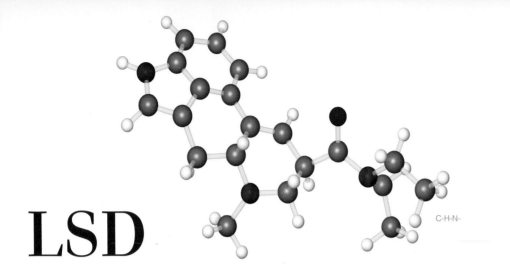

C·H·N·

1943

The very first LSD trip in the history of humankind was experienced by the Swiss chemist Albert Hofmann. He discovered the hallucinating effects of lysergic acid diethylamide when the substance was accidentally absorbed into his bloodstream via his fingertips. Initially, he wasn't impressed with the mixture that he had prepared from poisonous ergot to stimulate contractions. However, a "peculiar presentiment" made him return to the chemical. On April 19, 1943, three days after his first experience, he intentionally ingested 0.25 milligram of LSD in the name of science. The result is known as Bicycle Day: Hofmann was hardly able to return home on his bike and was besieged by hallucinations, panic attacks, paranoia, dizziness, and euphoria until deep into the night. He had hoped to use LSD with psychiatric patients, but even as the substance grew developed into a popular drug during the '60s, it became illegal almost worldwide.

Penicillin

1928

We owe the invention of the first antibiotic to the warm temperature in the laboratory of the Scottish scientist Alexander Fleming. In a small room in St. Mary's Hospital, in London, he experimented with bacteria from hospital patients. The boiler in the room next to his laboratory threw out so much heat that he often had to open a window, allowing dust, mold, and seeds to enter. On September 28, 1928, yet another petri dish with staphylococcus had been contaminated by mold. As he was about to clean the dish, he noticed that the bacteria around the green mold had disappeared. The mold itself appeared to release a substance that could kill bacteria, which Fleming called penicillin. Thanks to his discovery, which led the way for the creation of several other antibiotics, the era when people died from simple bacterial infections was history.

"The most exciting phrase to hear in science, the one that heralds new discoveries, is not 'Eureka!' but 'That's funny'..."

—Isaac Asimov (1920–1992), American writer and biochemist

Stethoscope

1816

We have the prudishness of a nineteenth-century French doctor to thank for the invention of the stethoscope. In the days of René Laënnec, doctors would hold their ear against the chest of their patient to diagnose an illness. When, in 1816, Laënnec was visited by a voluptuous young lady (who, according to some, lacked knowledge of basic hygiene), he was far from keen on placing his cheek to her chest. Suddenly, he remembered two children that morning playing by the Louvre: One of them had scratched with a needle at one end of a tree trunk, while the other was able to hear the amplified sound on the other side. He took a small pile of papers, shaped them into a funnel, and positioned it between his ear and the girl's chest. Never before had he heard chest sounds more clearly and with such volume. This inspired him to invent the stethoscope, still an essential instrument in the medical world today.

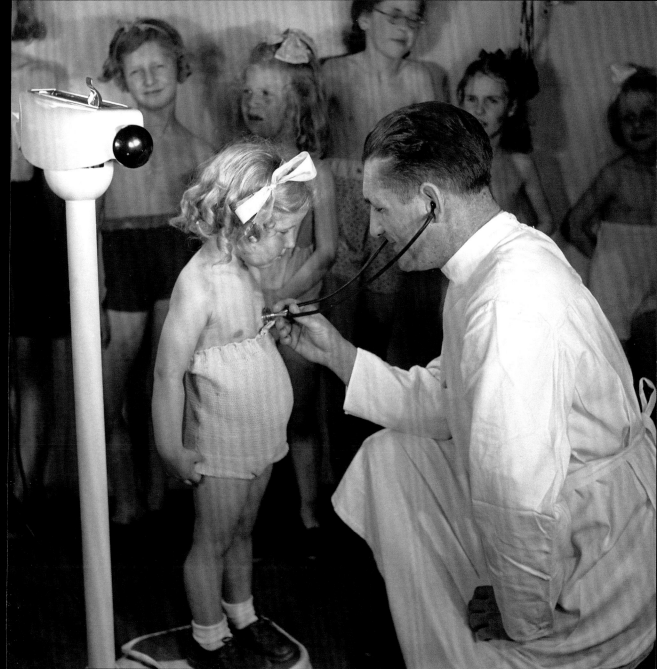

Viagra

Men with erection problems should not be hard on the researchers of Pfizer in Sandwich, England. It was they who in 1993 discovered that sildenafil citrate could decrease impotence. Although it was initially studied to treat angina, tests revealed it to be unsuccessful. However, male volunteers were soon successful in other areas: The substance seemed to increase the inflow of blood with sexual stimuli, enabling them to get and keep up an erection more easily. Pfizer immediately saw a gap in the market and altered the focus of the study. The introduction of Viagra in 1998 lead to a true revolution for impotent men. The blue diamond-shaped pill is still one of the top 100 most-sold drugs.

Band-Aids

1920

The invention of the adhesive bandage was a blessing in disguise. In 1920, when Earle Dickson married Josephine Knight in New Jersey, it soon became clear that his new wife was not to be trusted with knives. After a while, he was so fed up with having to dress new wounds every day with fiddly tape and disproportionately sized pieces of cotton gauze that he decided to precut some bandages, ready for his wife to apply herself. He folded gauze, stuck it to strips of tape and covered it with crinoline in order to avoid it sticking together. The invention worked, and his wife was delighted. The story would probably have come to an end here if it weren't for the fact that Dickson was a cotton buyer with the pharmaceutical company Johnson & Johnson. His boss, as excited as Josephine was, put Band-Aids into production and soon made Dickson vice president. It is impossible to imagine life today without self-adhesive bandages.

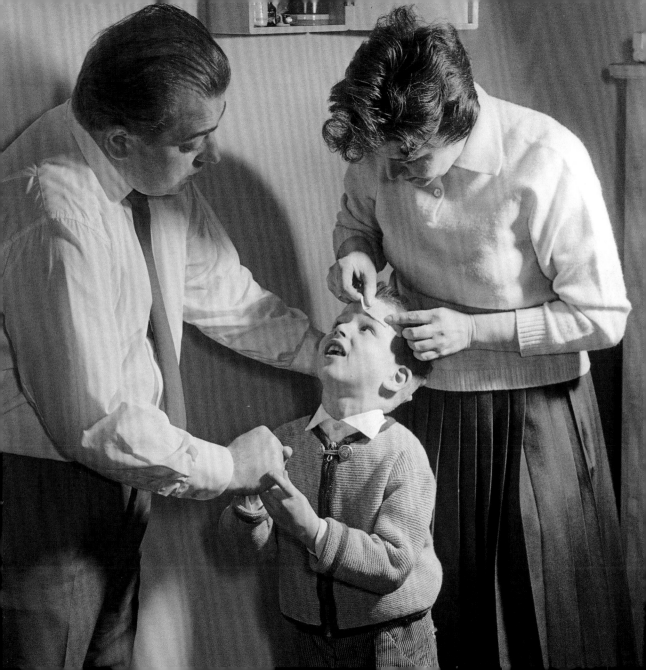

Rubber Gloves

The invention of the rubber glove was inspired by love. In 1889, when surgical nurse Caroline Hampton, from the Johns Hopkins Hospital, in Baltimore, suffered from eczema due to the liquids that she had to use to disinfect her hands and sterilize instruments. Chief surgeon William S. Halsted, who was madly in love with her, felt it an honor to resolve her problem. He sent a plaster cast of her hands to the Goodyear Rubber Company and ordered latex gloves that were resistant to heat and chemicals. His strategy worked: The eczema disappeared, and they married in 1890. Six years later, Halsted discovered that the sterile gloves were more efficient for controlling contact infection than the time-consuming chemical baths used at the time. He ordered himself some that were thinner and elastic, like a second skin. Since then, every surgeon has used rubber gloves, and in the early twentieth century, the gloves also started to appear in other fields such as the cleaning industry.

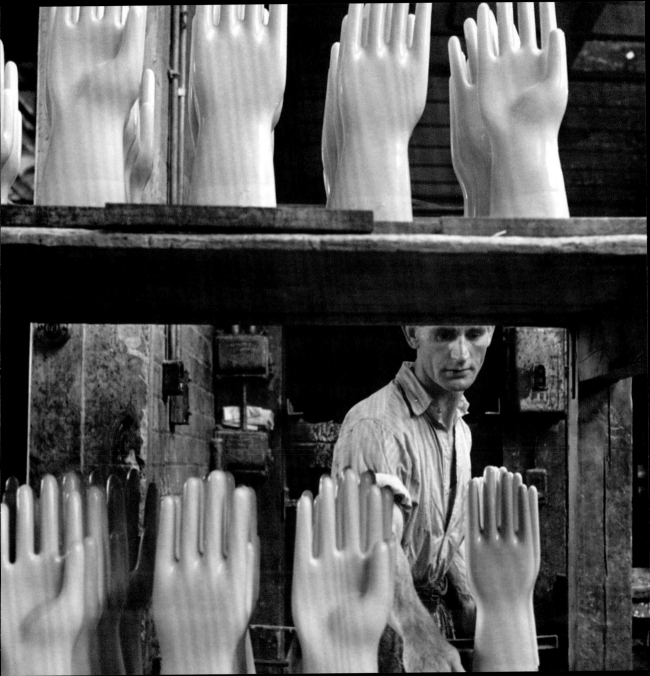

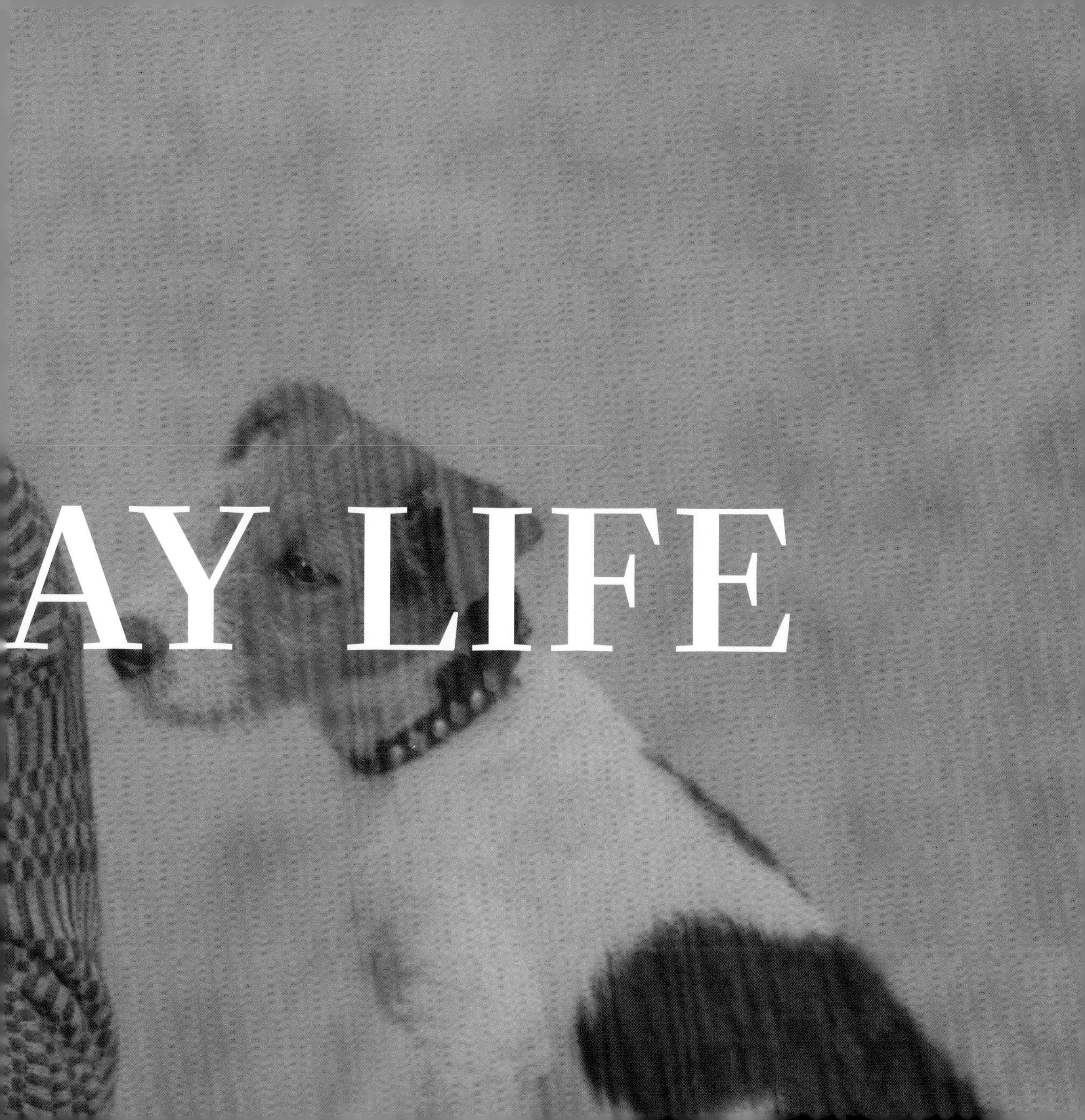
AY LIFE

Superglue

In 1942, chemist Harry Coover, from Kodak Laboratories, was desperately trying to find an ultratransparent type of plastic to use in precision gunsights when he investigated with cyanoacrylate. Fully unaware of the fact that he had just discovered one of the most versatile types of glue ever and frustrated by its fast action and extreme stickiness, he threw it away and carried on working. Only years later, during new research, he remembered the substance and realized its unique properties. Together with his team, he tried out the glue on all types of surfaces. Without fail, regardless of heat or pressure, the result was permanent adhesion. Although it was brought onto the market in 1958 under the name Eastman 910, it became widely known as Superglue.

Post-its

1980

In 1968, 3M scientist Spencer Silver was looking for a strong adhesive when he stumbled across a glue that hardly stuck at all and took an excruciatingly long time to dry. The product was put to rest in the 3M archives and would have stayed there if it had not been for Silver's colleague Arthur Fry. He sang in his church choir and was in search for a bookmark for his hymnal that would neither fall out nor damage it. Using Silver's glue, he produced small pieces of paper that temporarily adhered to the book. Convinced of the brilliance of his idea, he gave some samples to his colleagues. They hardly ever used them as bookmarks, though, but adopted them as a medium of communication. Written notes appeared in files, on telephones, and on doors. It wasn't until 1980, however, that the yellow squares made it onto the market. Currently, Post-its rank in the top five of most popular office supplies.

.

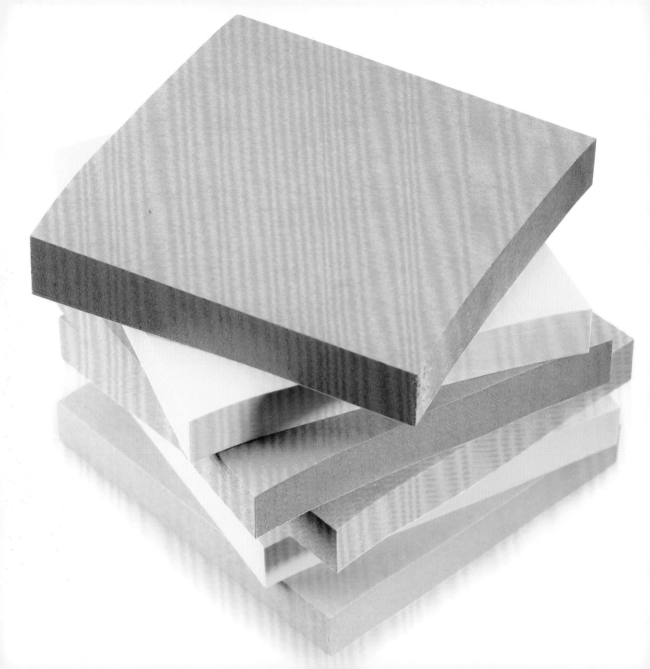

Safety Glass

1903

Laminated safety glass was accidentally discovered in 1903 by the French scientist Edouard Benedictus. He was standing on a ladder, taking ingredients for an experiment off a high shelf, when he dropped a glass flask. Much to his surprise, he discovered that the glass was shattered but the pieces still hung together, more or less in their original contour. His assistant confessed that he had placed the flask back unwashed after an experiment with nitrocellulose, which had evaporated in the bottle. Later, when Benedictus read in the newspaper about a girl who was seriously injured in a car accident by flying glass, he remembered the incident. He developed laminated glass, existing of two glass layers with a cellulose interlayer, and called his invention triplex. Safety glass was originally incorporated only in gas masks, but after World War I, it was also used in cars, aviation, and, more recently, the building industry.

Flashlight

1890

The first flashlight, a novelty item designed to be attached to a tie or scarf, was invented in 1896 by David Misell, an inventor who had previously created battery-powered portable and bicycle-mounted lamps. Misell, who went to work for New York City novelty-shop owner Conrad Hubert, took out a patent on it the next year, and Hubert introduced Misell's handheld flashlight in 1898.

Hubert had recently bought the American Eveready Battery Company from inventor Joshua Lionel Cowen, who later founded the Lionel Corporation, which originally produced novelty products but later branched off into model trains. The new owner, who renamed the firm the American Electrical Novelty & Manufacturing Company, distributed a few of the devices to the New York City Police Department, which provided glowing testimonials, and the flashlight soon became a worldwide sensation.

"My invention can be exploited ... as a scientific curiosity, but apart from that it has no commercial value whatsoever."

—Auguste Lumière about the
motion picture camera
he invented in 1895

Kleenex

The word Kleenex was not always a synonym for "disposable tissue." The main material, cellucotton, was originally used during World War I as a replacement for cotton in gas masks. In 1924, after the war, Kimberly-Clark marketed the material in the United States as facial tissues to remove makeup. Many letters were sent to the company by women who loved the product, but who found it unfortunate that their husbands and children used the tissues to blow their noses. When research indicated that approximately 60 percent of customers used Kleenex for this purpose, the product was launched for a third time, in 1930, as a disposable handkerchief. Sales doubled. All over the world, disposable tissues are now more popular than cotton handkerchiefs. Kleenex is made in 30 countries and marketed in more than 170.

Matches

1827 The first friction match is thought to have been created purely by accident. In 1827, the British chemist John Walker was trying to create a new explosive by mixing antimony sulfide and potassium chlorate, when he was called away from his laboratory. Upon his return, he noticed that the mixture had formed a hard lump on the stirrer. When he tried to remove it by scraping it over the floor, he was astonished to see the whole thing catch fire. The matchstick was born!

Walker's matches, which he called congreves, were soon in great demand, and when he died in 1859, he left a modest fortune, though, for humanitarian reasons, he had refused to patent his invention. Today, matches are made from different materials, but the concept still remains a hit: Worldwide, approximately 500 billion matches are used every year.

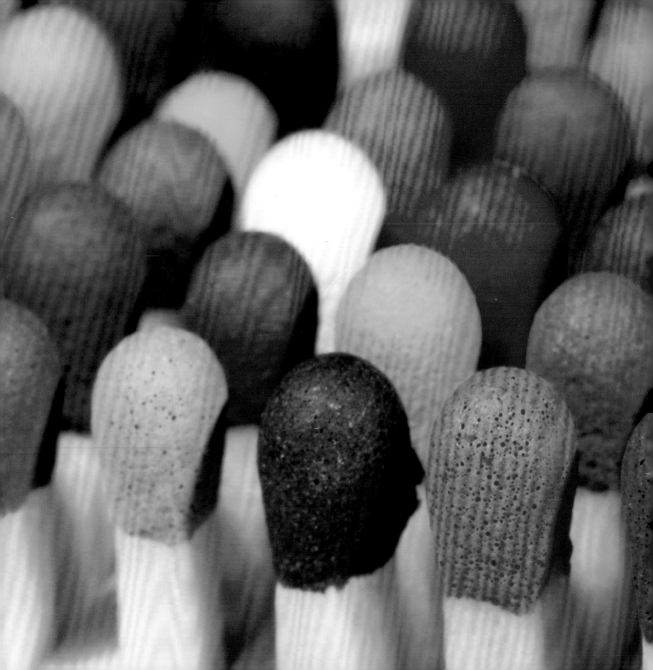

OBJECTS IN MIRROR ARE CLOSER THAN THEY APPEAR

Rear-View Mirror

1911

The rear-view mirror started its career on a race track. Early in the twentieth century, it was common practice for a mechanic to sit in the back of a racing car in order to keep an eye on pursuers. When, in 1911, Ray Harroun could not find anyone to join him in his Marmon race car during the Indianapolis 500 race, he installed a mirror on his car so he could see himself what was happening behind him. (Which was everything, because he won the race.) His invention was commercialized in 1914. Now, every car comes with a rear-view mirror as a standard accessory.

Guide Dog

It is not clear when exactly the idea arose for dogs to help out the blind. In the history of literature and art, several examples can be found referring to unique dogs helping their blind owners. However, it wasn't until World War I that the first guide-dog training schools were founded. Thousands of German soldiers were left visually impaired or blind during this war as a result of mustard gas attacks. When German doctor Gerhard Stalling was called away during a walk with one of his patients, he ordered his German Shepherd to keep the man company. He was surprised to see that the man and dog had continued their walk in his absence. Stalling realized this was the solution for the problem and in 1916 opened the world's first guide-dog training school. His concept became a standard for every such institution.

"Imagination is more important than knowledge."

—Albert Einstein (1879–1955),
German scientist and inventor

Velcro

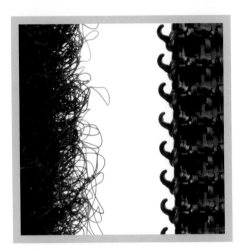

In 1941, electrical engineer Georges de Mestral wasn't looking for inspiration when he went on a hunting trip with his dog, but what he returned with would lead him to an invention that would change his life. The fur of this dog and his own socks had become covered in burrs of burdock. After he removed them with great difficulty, he examined one under a microscope and noted their hundreds of microscopic hooks that caught on anything with loops. De Mestral saw the possibility of a strong, lasting, and easy-to-use fastener. In 1949, he discovered that, when sewn under infrared light, nylon forms small but tough hooks that easily fasten onto soft polyester material. He called his invention velcro, after the French words *velours* (velvet) and *crochet* (hook). The revolutionary fastening system was commercialized in 1959 and is still used in a huge range of products.

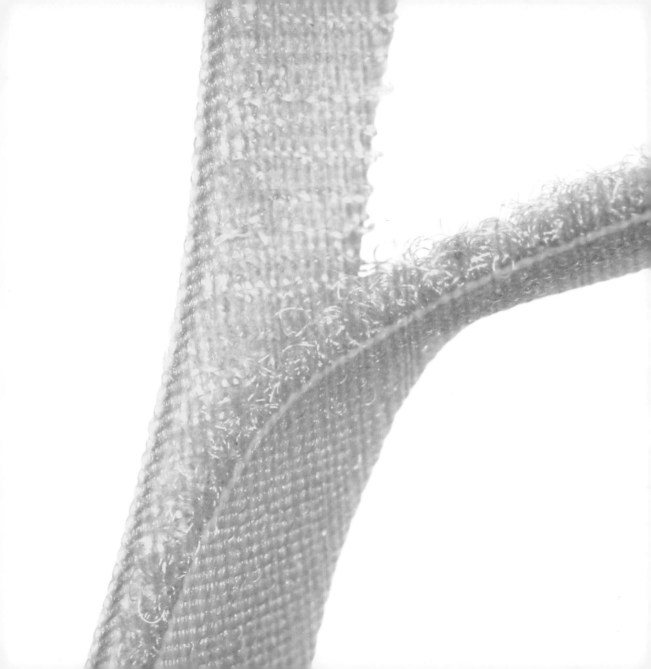

Blotting Paper

1465

Since the introduction of the ballpoint and, later on, the PC, blotting paper has become obsolete, but those of you who remember writing with an old-fashioned fountain pen at school will remember the pink sheets, full of inkblots, hidden in diaries and notebooks. According to a British legend, in 1465, this ultra-absorbent paper was accidentally invented when someone forgot to add glue to the paper mixture at the paper mill at Lyng Mill, in Norfolk. In the past, ink had been dried by sprinkling sand over the sheet of paper.

Abstract Art

1910

The well-known Russian expressionist painter Wassily Kandinsky is regarded as the founder of abstract painting. According to a popular anecdote, one evening when he arrived back home at his studio apartment in Munich, he noticed a strange and unrecognizable image of what he called "unusual inner beauty." He soon found out that it was one of his own figurative paintings standing upside down on an easel. It is said that this experience convinced him of the powers of full abstraction.

eBay

According to a popular Silicon Valley myth, the world's most famous online auction site owes its existence to Pez candy dispensers, which feature heads of toy and cartoon characters. In 1995, Pez fan Pam Wesley mentioned to her fiancé, Pierre Omidyar, that it was such a shame that she hadn't met any other Pez collectors yet since their move to Silicon Valley. This comment inspired the thoughtful IT professional to create an exchange site for her on the infant Internet, developing the code for what would later become eBay. The history of eBay remained as described above until in 2002, when the by-now-wealthy eBay founder had to admit that it had been a PR stunt and that the very first object traded via the site was not a Pez dispenser, but a broken laser pen.

World Wide Web

The founder of the World Wide Web created something much bigger than he had anticipated. The system of hypertext documents accessed through the Internet was set up in 1989 by computer programmer Tim Berners-Lee as a worldwide communication tool for the internal and external employees of the Swiss physics research laboratory CERN. As much of the information gathered was doomed to disappear in files no one ever looked in, he designed a program, HTML, that was able to link these reports using hypertext. He assumed that everyone had a computer with an Internet connection at their disposal but that the computers and operating systems varied greatly. On a whim, he decided to make the spider web technique available to everyone, on as many computers as possible all over the world. The World Wide Web has since grown into a global communication source that connects billions of computers.

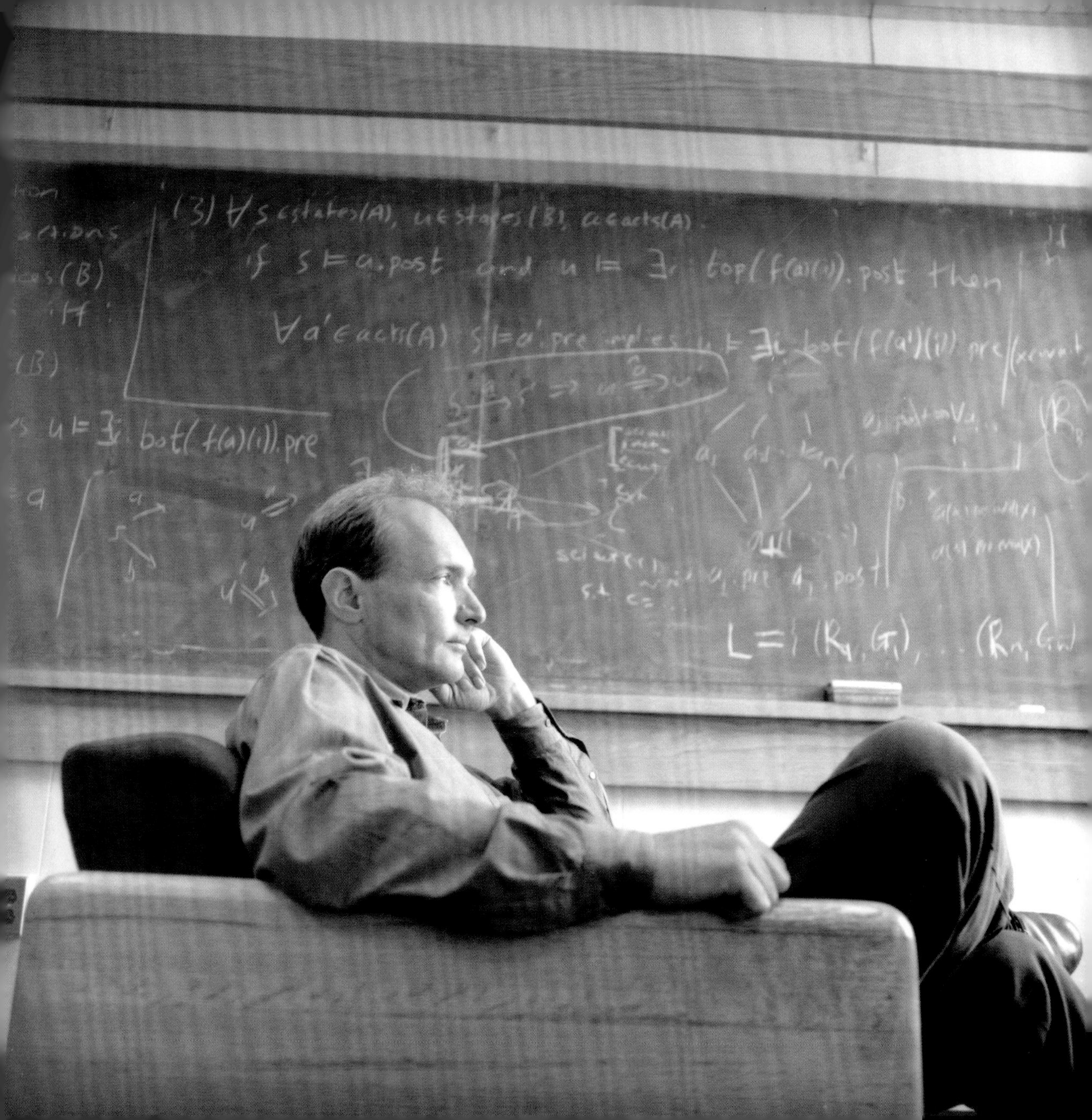
if s ⊨ a.post and u ⊨ ∃i top(f(a)(i)).post then
u ⊨ ∃i bot(f(a)(i)).pre

Phonograph

1877

Thomas Alva Edison wasn't sure what he was trying to invent when he discovered a way to reproduce sound on August 12, 1877. In an attempt to invent a machine that was able to record and replay telegraph messages, he had wrapped a cylinder with tinfoil and attached a funnel with a stylus. While the cylinder rotated using a winder, the stylus made indentations in the foil with the rhythm of the sound. After the excitement of several successful tests, he recited the opening verse of the nursery rhyme "Mary had a little lamb" into the machine, and to his great surprise, he heard his words replayed in his own voice. For a while, Edison assumed he had invented a tool to assist recording telephone conversations. In reality, the phonograph was a revolutionary invention that, as the prototype of the gramophone and later the record player and CD player, paved the way for an era of modern sound registration.

"Invention, in my opinion, arises directly from idleness, possibly also from laziness— to save oneself trouble."

—Agatha Christie, English mystery author (1890–1976)

Typewriter

The world's first practical commercially successful typewriter was invented as a machine to number pages. It took the American newspaper publisher and politician Christopher Latham Sholes several years of hard work to finally design such a machine when lawyer Carlos Glidden asked him point-blank why the thing wasn't able to type any letters. Sholes accepted the challenge, slaved away for a further five years, and in 1872 delivered a useable typewriter that was commercialized the year after by the weapon and sewing machine manufacturer Remington. Although the typewriter wasn't an immediate success, it lay the foundations for the global automation of office work by enabling switching from handwritten to typed and electronic documents. The QWERTY keyboard, worked out by Sholes to avoid frequently used keys from clashing, is still standard in most countries using the Latin alphabet.

Bubble Wrap

Bubble wrap was originally invented as a new type of wallpaper. In 1957, in a garage in New Jersey, the American engineer Al Fielding and Swiss inventor Marc Chavannes tried to create a wall covering with easy-to-hang paper at the back and easy-to-clean relief plastic on the front. The results were flexible plastic sheets with bubbles that weren't exactly aesthetically pleasing but were practical: They were ideal as wrapping material. Bubble wrap was commercialized in 1960 by Sealed Air Corporation as a means of protection for fragile objects. Everywhere, people still use bubble wrap as a wrapping material and enjoy popping bubbles as a source of amusement.

Teflon

1938

In 1930, DuPont chemist Roy Plunkett accidentally invented Teflon when attempting to make a new coolant. The American used tetrafluoroethylene gas in his experiments that he had produced in large quantities and stored using dry ice. On the morning of April 6, 1938, as he was about to start a new experiment, he noticed that the pressure in the cylinder had dropped. The gas could not have escaped, as the weight of the cylinder remained unchanged. Frustrated, he removed the valve, turned the cylinder over, and, to his astonishment, saw a smooth white powder pour out. The gas had polymerized to a substance that we now know as Teflon. A number of years later, during World War II, Teflon was used for gaskets and valves in armor. After that, it made its entry into every kitchen in the world as nonstick coating for pans.

Cellophane

1908

Cellophane, the transparent wrapping material that is mainly used for food, was accidentally invented by the Swiss textile engineer Jacques Brandenberger. One evening when he was out for dinner, he witnessed a glass of red wine ruining a linen table-cloth and decided that he was going to invent a waterproof and stain-free table cover. When he added a layer of liquid viscose onto a cloth during one of his experiments, it instantly became stiff and breakable. After the experiment, Brandenberger noticed that the layer could be peeled off like a transparent foil. By 1908, he had created a machine that was able to produce sheets of viscose. Cellophane has been produced since the 1930s and is still used to hermetically pack food and in a number of industrial applications.

Stainless Steel

1913 Although many scientists were experimenting with steel alloying in the same period, the Englishman Harry Brearley is considered the inventor of stainless steel. While looking for a corrosion-resistant alloy for gun barrels and cannons in 1913, the metallurgist at Brown Firth Research Laboratories, in Sheffield, noticed how one of the rejected barrels, in comparison to all others, was not corroded. The alloy consisted of 12.8 percent chromium and 0.24 percent carbon, a new magic formula that, after bonding with oxygen, forms an invisible layer of dichromium trioxide, which protects the underlying layer of metal against corrosion and repairs itself when damaged. It was not in the least suited for the arms industry but is, nearly 100 years later, still used in the catering, medicine, and transport industries.

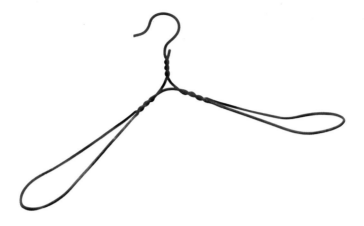

Wire Coat Hanger

The wire coat hanger was invented because the Timberlake Wire and Novelty Company, specializing in making frames for lampshades, had a shortage of coat hooks. In 1903, when employee Albert J. Parkhouse arrived late at work one day and all coat hooks had been taken, he instinctively grabbed some wire, bent two large hoops facing each other, and turned the ends into a hook, then hung up his coat and got to work. Timberlake thought this was a stroke of genius and took out a patent on the construction. The company made a fortune with the coat hangers, while Parkhouse was left with nothing.

⑤ SUBSTA

NCES

TNT

TNT made its entry into the world as a yellow dye. In 1863, the German chemist Julius Wilbrand was the first person to successfully produce trinitrotoluene through the nitration of toluene. The result was a pretty yellow dye that—aside from its extreme poisonousness—had no flaws. As it could be ignited only by using a detonator, it wasn't until 1902 that the destructive power of TNT became known. Today, the substance, which can be safely poured in liquid form into shell cases, is still used for military purposes.

Radioactivity

1856

Radioactivity is not exactly the word you would like to associate with the exclamation "Oops, slight problem!" but it's a fact that it was discovered by accident. In 1856, Henri Becquerel was intrigued by the invention of X-rays and wanted to prove that this phenomenon had the same cause as the glow produced by certain salts after exposure to light (fluorescence). This theory was confirmed when, during an experiment, a clear imprint appeared after he placed a uranium salt crystal in sunlight on top of a wrapped photographic plate. However, when the sun disappeared during subsequent experiments, Becquerel decided to store the mineral sample and the plate in a drawer. When he developed the plate a few days later after all, he noticed to his surprise that it had entirely blackened. It soon became clear that fluorescence had nothing to do with radiation. He had to draw the conclusion that uranium was able to produce a new type of invisible radiation. Becquerel had discovered radioactivity.

"I didn't plan to make the Cube."

—Erno Rubik, inventor of the Rubik's Cube in 1974

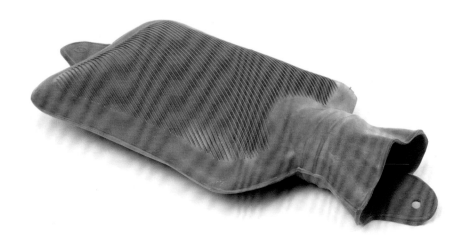

Vulcanized Rubber

1839

Rubber was an exciting but especially difficult substance when it was first introduced in 1736 in France: The potential was enormous, but it became sticky when hot and rock hard when cold, stunk like a skunk and decomposed quickly. It was Charles Goodyear, from Ohio, who in 1839 discovered vulcanization due to his own clumsiness. For eight fruitless years, he had been researching methods to make the material more manageable when he accidentally spilled a mixture of rubber and sulfur on a hot stove. The material melted but kept its elasticity and became stronger and far less sticky. His discovery of the vulcanization process led not only to the use of rubber tires in the car industry but also to the invention of a number of other rubber products.

Scotchgard

1952

Patsy Sherman is the first to admit that inventions can result from silly incidents. The 3M scientist was one of only a few women in her field when, in 1952, she was teamed up with colleague Sam Smith to search for a new type of rubber for the fuel pipes of fighter planes. One day, she dropped a bottle of synthetic latex she had made next to one of her assistant's white fabric tennis shoes. To her astonishment, the substance did not change the look of the material; however, it was impossible to remove it. Moreover, the material had become waterproof and stain free. In 1956, the water- and stain-repellent spray hit the market. As the spray could be used on not only clothing and shoes but also carpets, upholstery, and other materials, 20 varieties were developed. Today, 3M's Scotchgard is still the world's market leader in fabric protection.

Synthetic Dyes

Teenage student William Perkin managed to turn the textile industry upside down when he invented the world's first synthetic dye during a failed experiment. Before his discovery, dyes came from nature and were rare, expensive, and hardly wash resistant. Initially, Perkin had no interest in the matter; encouraged by his teacher at London's Royal College of Chemistry, he was trying to invent a synthetic form of the medicine quinine. After one of his experiments had failed again during Easter break in 1856, he was left with a reaction flask full of black slush. As he started to clean everything up using alcohol, he noticed that the slush dissolved and the alcohol turned purple. In all his excitement, he soaked a cloth in the substance and gaped at the intense purple color a few minutes later. He left school, patented mauveine, started up a company, and was wealthy by the age of 21. His discovery was the onset for the invention of thousands of other dyes.

Dynamite

1866

Nitroglycerin is not a substance to play with. Alfred Nobel had come to that conclusion in 1864 when his younger brother Emil died in an explosion during one of their experiments. Two years later, the Swedish chemist had a breakthrough when, trying to stabilize this liquid explosive, he spilled a few drops on the floor. Luckily for him, no real damage was done, and he found out that the absorption by porous materials dramatically decreases the sensitivity of the liquid. The result he called dynamite. A few years after Nobel's discovery, dynamite was the most-used explosive in the world, employed for building railways, harbors, bridges, roads, mines, and tunnels. (And, yes, he instituted the Nobel prizes.)

"**Everything that can be invented has been invented.**"

—Charles H. Duell, commissioner of the US Patent Office, in 1899 when he disclosed that he wanted to close down the patent office.

"Books may well be the only true magic."

—Alice Hoffman, American author